fast
thinking:
de-stress

PEARSON EDUCATION LIMITED

Head Office:
Edinburgh Gate
Harlow CM20 2JE
Tel: +44 (0)1279 623623
Fax: +44 (0)1279 431059

London Office:
128 Long Acre
London WC2E 9AN
Tel: +44 (0)20 7447 2000
Fax: +44 (0)20 7240 5771
Website: www.fast-thinking.com

First published in Great Britain in 2002

The right of Richard Templar to be identified as Author
of this Work has been asserted by him in accordance
with the Copyright, Designs and Patents Act 1988.

ISBN 0 273 65480 2

British Library Cataloguing in Publication Data
A CIP catalogue record for this book can be obtained from the British Library

10 9 8 7 6 5 4 3 2 1

Typeset by Pantek Arts Ltd, Maidstone, Kent
Printed and bound in Great Britain by Ashford Colour Press, Hampshire

The Publishers' policy is to use paper manufactured from sustainable forests.

fast
thinking:
de-stress

- ▶ **lose tension**
- ▶ **feel relaxed**
- ▶ **cope better**

by Richard Templar

contents

introduction

OK, so you've been in this job a while now and things are getting out of hand. Your stress levels are rising and there never seems to be any time to do anything about it. You've got tense shoulders, a tight feeling in your chest and you're irritable and anxious. Things may have got so bad you're thinking of leaving. You're at breaking point and ready to chuck in the towel.

But hold up a moment. Even if you do leave and go to a new job, chances are that nothing will really improve. What you need to do is learn how to cope with the stress, improve your approach to it and find ways of reducing it. If you can't change the situation, change your response.

Most of us find that our stress is caused by one of three things:

- ▶ **People**
- ▶ **Ourselves**
- ▶ **Work.**

Yep, a pretty powerful knock-out blow for most of us. Pow! So what you need is an express guide to zip you through quick and practical solutions to all of these stressful problems. And you've just found it. *fast thinking: de-stress* is the guide for you. It contains only quick solutions, which are easy to learn, fun to carry out and, most importantly of all, effective.

Getting rid of your stress completely isn't possible, or even desirable – you'd be like a deflated balloon – but what certainly is possible is to give you a breathing space to stand back and assess the situation in a calmer and more relaxed way. Once we can create that space we can actually see clearly:

- ▶ **what is causing the stress**
- ▶ **how to alleviate it now**
- ▶ **how to manage it long term**
- ▶ **how to stop it recurring.**

If you don't take steps now to reduce your stress levels it will affect your work, your health, your relationships and your career. By dealing with it now you will find work more enjoyable, easier to manage and infinitely preferable to chucking in the towel and admitting defeat. What you need is:

- ▶ **speedy information about what makes us stressed**
- ▶ **tips and shortcuts for getting on top of stress fast**
- ▶ **guidelines for easing future stress**
- ▶ **checklists to monitor and reduce your stress levels fast**

... all put together clearly and simply. And short enough to read fast, of course. You've come to the right place.

What if you've got to deal with a really stressful situation immediately, such as an interview scheduled for right now? Well, we can still help. At the back of the book you'll find ways of de-stressing yourself in half an hour and, if you're really up against the pressure, a guide to de-stressing in ten minutes. Now that really is thinking at the speed of life.

So chill for a moment and take a deep breath. You may be feeling totally stressed out and ready to blow, but help is at hand. You're going to de-stress, and de-stress fast. You're going to be left feeling calm and collected, on top of it all, in charge, cool and looking relaxed – while still firing on all cylinders.

key points

DE-STRESS AT THE SPEED OF LIFE

This book will guide you through the five key stages of dealing with stress:

1 Figuring out the cause of stress – before you can learn what causes stress or how to deal with it, you have to know why you are embarking on this exercise – what you want to achieve and why. This is a quick and easy thing to do and is known as *setting your objective* – identifying what you are going to get out of all this de-stressing.

2 Alleviating stress from other people's interruptions – all the tips and techniques you'll need to ease the pain and deal effectively with them all, stopping those interruptions – now!

3 Problems with other people – we might not be able to change everybody, the petty people, the difficult people, the boring people, the rude people and obstructive colleagues, but we can change our response. This chapter will tell you how – and fast.

4 Problems with some specific tricky types – we'll tell you how to deal with the sulky ones, the angry ones and the bosses, of course.

5 Alleviating stress from work – tips and techniques for easing workloads, restructuring work schedules, learning to say 'no', beating the system, organising time better, reducing the stress from nerves and simply working more effectively, faster and more efficiently. And being kind to ourselves, of course.

You may be feeling totally stressed out and ready to blow, but help is at hand. You're going to de-stress, and de-stress fast

fast thinking gambles

So, you can learn to alleviate and combat stress fast and effectively, but there are risks. If you follow the guidelines in this book you won't go far wrong; you'll be calmer, more relaxed, happier both at home and at work, and you'll generally feel better and fitter. But there is always a risk when you do things as fast as we are going to:

- ▶ You've cleared so much space and are so relaxed you see that you would be happier elsewhere anyway and leave despite all the good work we are going to do.

- ▶ You concentrate so much on alleviating the symptoms of stress that you overlook a vital health issue (but we will be prepared for that and have lots of information on spotting serious ill-health warning signs).

- ▶ There are also longer-term/slower approaches, some of which can go deep. You don't want to miss out by being in too much of a hurry.

Fast thinking will get you unknotted, de-stressed, relaxed and looking good at speed and you'll end up a more effective team member, better equipped to deal with anything those b*****ds can throw at you – and a damn sight happier. Not only will you be doing a better job but you'll be whistling as you go and spreading a little happiness all around you. Stressed people attract stress – people like to kick you when you are down. Chilled people, on the other hand, cope much better because they take it all in their stride and thus attract less stress. Let's do it. Let's do it now before it gets worse.

1 your objective

Have we got time for this? Surely we are all so stressed that we need to get on with de-stressing and learning to be more relaxed. Yep. Good point. But if we don't set an objective, how can we measure our success? By setting an objective we can identify where our stress is coming from, take steps to alleviate it and set in motion changes in behaviour and patterns to stop it getting worse and to prevent it occurring again.

To do all that we have to understand exactly what we mean by stress. And the first thing is to acknowledge that *pressure* and *stress* are not the same thing. We need deadlines to keep us focused. We need a challenge at work to keep us motivated, interested and stimulated. We need pressure to make us feel alive and keen. What we don't need is stress. And stress isn't having deadlines; it's having deadlines that are unrealistic.

Having lots of work isn't stress, but having too much work is. Having a busy and challenging work environment isn't stress, but having a work environment where we feel unsupported, surrounded by ineffectual and rude colleagues, and generally isolated and unthanked is stress.

CHANGING YOURSELF

Now, apart from quitting your job, there isn't too much you can do about changing everyone and everything else. So your objective must be to change *yourself* so you cope better and are less affected by what goes on around you. You need to find new and quick ways of alleviating the symptoms of stress as well as ways of feeling more in control and more assertive about how you handle your work.

KEEP THE PRESSURE, DUMP THE STRESS

Your objective must be to get rid of the stress while keeping the pressure. You can't have an easy, lazy work life or you will simply stagnate and stop progressing. You need to be challenged, stimulated, stretched, encouraged and motivated. You won't get that by coasting. The answer to alleviating stress isn't more time off, better and longer holidays, less work or nicer people. The answer to alleviating stress is to change your response so that the stress doesn't affect you as much and you have the gumption to stop the things that stress you occurring in the first place. A tall order indeed, but easier to achieve than some Utopian fantasy where everything is really easy, really chilled, really smooth. It ain't going to happen, kiddo. Better to live in the real world and survive than to dream a fiction and fail.

So our objective is to find:

- **ways to cope better**
- **ways to stop stressful things occurring**
- **fast and effective techniques to combat stress now.**

You can now spend a few minutes writing that down and propping it up in front of you on your desk:

My objective is to find fast ways to enable me to cope better and to cut down on the stressful situations.

THE TWO-PRONGED APPROACH

You are in effect setting up a two-pronged attack:

1. **You will change yourself by changing your responses.**
2. **You will change the situation by changing your responses.**

Having set your objective you can measure any action you intend taking against this objective. Suppose your real stress lies in other people – interruptions, rudeness, petty squabbles, incompetence, ineffectiveness, you name it. What are you going to do about it? Well, now you have your objective you can easily see that 'other people,' isn't a situation and thus vulnerable to attack number 2. So you will use attack number 1 – change yourself.

It's not me, it's them

I know, I know. It ain't you; it's all the other tossers. But you simply can't change them all. In fact, I doubt if you could even change some of them. And if the truth is known you ain't even gonna change one of them. So changing yourself, changing your responses, is the only logical thing to do. By simply ceasing to be affected you'll outlive them all – and that is real success. We'll deal with the stressful *situations* these people create a bit later on – and deal with them effectively and fast – but for the moment take great comfort in the thought that you are going to be superior to them, you are going to learn how to let them wash over you like water off a duck's back. The little pools of misery and darkness that they form around them are going to be as nothing to you.

Now you have your objective you can begin the real work of dealing quickly with any stressful situation or person you encounter at work – and at home if you want to.

for next time

FOR NEXT TIME

There won't be a next time. You have your objective now which will last you for ever. The stress may come at you from different places, different things, but the fundamental principles will always be the same – change your response. Next time you will have stopped the stressful situation worsening before it upsets you and you will have learned how to change yourself so you are less affected by it.

By simply ceasing to be affected you'll outlive them all – and that is real success

2 handling interruptions

According to a recent business survey on the top reasons why people suffer stress at work, 'handling interruptions' rated in the top four. How can you get on with your own work if you are subjected to a constant barrage of interruptions from other people? The answer is that you can't. And thus you get stressed. Deadlines get missed, work gets done badly and your nerves get more and more ragged by the day. You have to act now, act fast to stop this high-stress cause. And to do so you may have to be a bit ruthless.

Dropping hints doesn't work. You have to spell it out clearly and forcefully. And that goes not only for the people popping their head round the office door for a chat but also for the e-mails, the phone calls, and the pointless meetings.

BEING PRODUCTIVE AND DETERMINED

Now before we can get on with the real work of stopping those interruptions you have to decide what it is you want from work. Is it to be a stressed manager with all the symptoms of neglect and abuse such as insomnia, tiredness, shortness of temper, constant niggling illnesses, headaches, smoking and/or drinking too much, an inability to relax? Or a lean, mean fighting machine? Smart team members take steps to make sure their stress levels stay low and thus they are geared up and ready for anything. They are productive and determined, dedicated and focused. Is that you? If it isn't then these tips and techniques won't work because *you* will be too hesitant to put them to good use. If you are ready for the challenge and really prepared to go for it, then we're in with a chance. But *you* have to decide. *You* have to be committed to serious action to become more effective, slicker and quicker, leaner and meaner, but kinder in the long run. If you stop these interruptions now, chances are the other people may go and get on with some work of their own.

If you are ready for the challenge and really prepared to go for it, then we're in with a chance. But you have to decide

HOW STRESSED ARE YOU?

Between you and that first breakdown or complete burnout there are usually four distinct phases. It is important to know where you are so you can take appropriate action – before it gets worse.

Phase 1: you suffer from too much energy, you overwork, feel over-conscientious, doubts begin to creep in about your ability to cope and you compensate by taking on more. You are too busy to take holidays and are reluctant to even take a day off. You take work home with you. You never have any time for your family. You get easily frustrated. *Action: take a break.*

STOPPING THE NONSENSE E-MAILS

It happens to us all. We come into the office in the morning and log on, only to find 27 e-mails waiting for us. Twenty-six of these are nonsense. The other one reminds us of an important meeting but it takes us nearly half an hour to wade through the garbage first – and that's time we can ill afford to lose. Let's stop this now. And fast.

Write an e-mail now to circulate to everyone (but not your boss, of course) who is in the habit of sending you junk e-mails. It should be short and pithy, to the point without actually being rude:

My e-mail facility is a work tool. I find I am wasting a lot of time reading unnecessary e-mails. Please could you not send me jokes, round robins, gossip, porno pictures, the latest spoof viruses, save the anything campaigns, chain letters, amusing animations and anything else that may not be work related.

II

thinking smart

HOW STRESSED ARE YOU?

Between you and that first breakdown or complete burnout there are usually four distinct phases. It is important to know where you are so you can take appropriate action – before it gets worse.

Phase 2: you get irritated easily and suffer from tiredness and feelings of being overwhelmed. You find it easy to blame others. You feel increasingly unable to cope with the pressure of work and you find yourself working overly long hours. You lose your ability to manage time effectively.

Action: take a big break.

You may get a reputation for being terribly serious and not a lot of fun but be assured this will only last a day or two and then people will simply exclude you from the nonsense e-mails, which is what you want. Send this circular e-mail to friends, colleagues and even relatives to ensure that when you come in there will be only the one important email waiting for you. You have to regard your e-mail facility as an important work tool in just the same way that a brain surgeon would regard their scalpel – you wouldn't ask to borrow it to do some lino cuts or sharpen your pencil. Your computer is your scalpel and shouldn't be used as a plaything.

So you might as well delete all those games now too. Yep, games are time suckers. They will fritter away time like nothing else – apart from surfing the web, that is – and should be erased. I know it's hard when you've become addicted to *Solitaire* or *InterGalaticWarriors* or whatever. But games deflect you from your true purpose – being a leaner, hungrier manager. Once you squander time on anything that isn't work, you leave less time for deadlines. Thus you get stressed. Get rid of anything that sucks time.

CAUSES AND CLASSIFICATIONS OF STRESS

There are five quite separate classifications of stress and it is important to know what sort of stress is affecting you. If you know, then perhaps you won't blame work quite so much – or maybe it really is the cause of all your stress.

- ▶ Individual stress – this is your own personal stress that you carry with you no matter what job you do or where you happen to be working.

- ▶ Interpersonal stress – this is stress caused by the way you react to people around you. This can be work relationships but can also be personal relationships.

- ▶ Systemic stress – this is caused by working/living in a system that fails to support you.

- ▶ Social stress – this is caused by the environment we live in. It includes cultural stress, national stress, community stress and international stress.

- ▶ Universal stress – this is stress that affects us all in one way or another, no matter what race or ethnic group we belong to. It includes things such as fear of dying, fear of long-term illness and spiritual dilemmas.

Games deflect you from your true purpose – being a leaner, hungrier manager. Once you squander time on anything that isn't work, you leave less time for deadlines

PHONE CALL INTERRUPTIONS

You're just sitting down to do your budgets or work on your presentation or put together the new sales exhibition stands when the phone rings and it's a colleague phoning for a chat or a bit of advice or just to confirm a meeting, and you're off and gabbling away and before you know it an hour has just slipped past. Now you're rushed, pressured, stressed. Solution? Easy. When you need space, put on your voice-mail facility. Switch on your answer phone. And don't listen in until you've finished that vital task.

If you find that you get a lot of phone interruptions, try putting on your voice mail and only picking up messages twice a day. People will soon twig that you are unavailable.

'Consider me prompted'

You can also try the brisk, urgent voice. Speak quicker. Be brusque and clipped to convey the impression that you are frightfully busy and very rushed. I once phoned a publisher to see if he had received a proposal of mine, and had he read it, and what did he think of it – that sort of thing. Really I was ringing for a chat and to sound him out. I began by asking if he had received the proposal. He answered, 'Yes, consider me prompted', and then hung up. For a while I didn't even understand what he meant. When I did, I realised he would then read the proposal and that he was frightfully busy and terribly important. Several years later when I had got to know him better, I asked him about it and he explained that it was simply a technique he used to cut off phone calls quickly when he was busy. And it worked, believe you me. It took me a long time to summon up the courage to phone him again.

His other technique was to respond with one- or two-word answers. I had to phone him to ask permission to change some things in a book I was working on. I outlined what I wanted to do and he merely said, 'Justify', which I then did – and did quickly as I was instantly made aware of how busy he obviously was. 'Do it', he said and hung up. Brilliant. Short. Quick. Intimidating. And conveys the air of extreme decisiveness. Brilliant.

Doing it standing up is quicker

If you do have to take phone calls, try talking while standing up. That'll shorten them. There is something urgent about the need to hang up when you are standing up. If you do get engrossed in a

HOW STRESSED ARE YOU?

Between you and that first breakdown or complete burnout there are usually four distinct phases. It is important to know where you are so you can take appropriate action – before it gets worse.

Phase 3: your irritation is turning to actual anger and you suffer from low self-esteem. You feel apathetic and guilty about how much time you fritter away. You have stopped enjoying much about work or your social life and you feel exhausted most of the time. You don't have any time for personal relationships and don't care about them. *Action: see a counsellor.*

long chat, just stand up and you'll be surprised how easy it is to finish a phone call quicker while doing so.

You can also say, 'Can we discuss this over lunch?' if it isn't important. And don't forget the fabulous old stand-by, 'Can I phone you back?'. But don't specify when.

BEING ASSERTIVE ON THE PHONE

You may need to be somewhat assertive to get rid of people on the phone, and this isn't something we are all good at. Remember though that it is an act of kindness, not cruelty, to cut them short. The quicker you are with them, the greater the chances are that they may then go off and do something useful with their time. Of course they may choose not to, and go off and bother someone else – but at least they aren't wasting *your* time.

thinking smart

HOW STRESSED ARE YOU?

Between you and that first breakdown or complete burnout there are usually four distinct phases. It is important to know where you are so you can take appropriate action – before it gets worse.

Phase 4: you are withdrawn and feel ill a lot of the time. You feel like a failure and have taken to avoiding going to work at all and communicating with anyone. You feel isolated and have stopped caring sufficiently for yourself. You may have taken to using alcohol to compensate or even drugs. *Action: see a doctor immediately.*

You may need to be somewhat assertive to get rid of people on the phone, and this isn't something we are all good at

LEAVING NOT EVICTING

Try to arrange informal 'meetings' in other people's rooms or offices – it's easier to get away than to evict them once they've got their feet under your desk. So if they call and say, 'Can I pop across and see you?' you can reply, 'I'll come and see you – I'll be there in ten minutes (or whatever time you need)'.

GETTING THEM OUT OF YOUR OFFICE

Of course, one of the hardest things to do is get someone out of your office. They may have time to kill but you don't. And they may not be there to help you with your work but to explore some agenda of their own which people often find hard to shut off without causing offence. So the door opens and your heart sinks. It's them again. You know they will stay and chat and you have an urgent deadline to meet. So, what are you going to do? Be rude and tell them to eff off? No. That merely sets up more problems for the future. No. You are going to handle them. But first you have to identify them. And there are five basic types of interrupter.

- ▶ **The egotist** – they drop by to tell you how wonderful they are. They boost their own ego by trying to get you to admire them; inflate their self-esteem by making you feel inadequate. They're not there to help you with your work but to feed off you. And the way to get rid of them is to cut off their food supply. If they come to boast about their latest achievement, just say, 'Yep, I had heard how brilliantly you'd pulled off that exhibition/finalised that new contract/made that awesome sale, but I am very busy just now. Us lesser mortals have to work much harder than you naturally gifted superstars. Could we meet over coffee later and you can tell me all about it then, huh?' That should shut them up for a bit – just so long as you aren't too sarcastic – but you will have to listen to them some time. Just make sure it is on your terms and not theirs.

- ▶ **The rambler** – they may have come to tell you something important but never quite seem to be able to get around to saying it. They talk too much, have little to say that is actually of any importance, veer from the point and generally ramble. You need to get them to cut to the chase and then go. But it's hard as they are immune to hints. They've been here before and know all the tricks – others have tried to shut them up. This one can only really be silenced by silence – or being truly assertive, which we will deal with a little later on. So stop answering. Stop talking to them. Be busy. Get up and walk around a lot as if you aren't paying any attention. Punctuate their ramble with lots of 'yeah, yeah', and 'uh ha' and 'mmm'. Open your filing cabinet

They boost their own ego by trying to get you to admire them; inflate their self-esteem by making you feel inadequate. They're not there to help you with your work but to feed off you and lose yourself in its interesting depths. Make a phone call or two. Look at your computer screen and type furiously. Look at your watch – a lot. Eventually they will get the message that you are one of those terrible types who simply won't give them any air space. They will get the message because they have had it before.

The humorist – they have nothing better to do than come and tell you their latest joke; entertain you with tales of their disgusting behaviour at the sales conference – after all, it is so funny (not); play practical jokes on you; try to get you involved with their latest jape – 'Come on, let's go and let off all the fire alarms, it will be such a gas.' It won't. With the humorist you have to be very serious. Don't laugh at anything they say, not even a smile should cross your lips. Refuse to be drawn into any japes, gags, jokes, stunts, hoaxes or pranks. As well as being assertive you have to give off the air of someone for whom all this is beneath them. You have to play the parent to their child. They will feel embarrassed – eventually – and leave you in peace. They may consider you a spoilsport, an old fuddy-duddy, a wet blanket, but chances are you will still be working long after they've been fired for some prank that got out of hand. Dissociate yourself from them, which can be hard as invariably they are funny and very entertaining. You could always try socialising with them outside of working hours but keep your distance in the office.

The time waster – and it's their time they are wasting as well as yours. They have nothing to do so they think dropping in on you is a simply brilliant way to pass a few hours. They're in your office faster than you can believe, got their feet under the table and are eating all your digestive biscuits before you've had a chance to stop them. They are neither use nor ornament and you can't shift them, they're here to stay. You need to be assertive, but you can also get rid of them quite quickly if you encourage them to run errands for you, help you with your work – 'Could you just file these for me, Bob, if you're here for a minute or two?' 'Ah, Bob, I'm really pleased to see you as I need all these figures checking, glad you dropped by.' They'll stop if you do make use of them. After all, the only reason they are there is to get out of their own office to avoid having to do any work.

(▶) **The gossip** – they simply have to poke their head round your door to make sure you've heard the latest about Mandy and that new sales director or what Tony was really doing in the boardroom with those two security officers. The gossip interrupter is quite hard to stop as we are all intrigued by tittle-tattle and they do present their information in such an intriguing way. It is so easy when someone says, 'Hey, have you heard about Sandra and the car park attendant being caught on CCTV?' to say, 'No, what happened?' Instead you have to be quite curt. 'Not now, Leslie, I'm frightfully busy getting these sales figures out. Could you tell me later?' Don't show any sign of being intrigued, interested or desperate to know. Chances are that you'll hear later anyway or that Sandra wasn't doing anything nearly as interesting as you'd like to think. And don't try saying, 'Yeah, I heard all about it'. They'll immediately demand to know what you think about it, how long's it been going on, who else knows, what you think the ramifications will be – that sort of thing. Don't give them an inch unless you really have the time to spare – allow at least an hour.

There are other types of interrupter but they are usually a combination of two or more of these five basic types. Once you've got a reputation for being serious, busy and diligent you get left alone a lot more often. Trouble is, we all want to be liked and to be popular, and being serious and hard working cuts us out from the herd. You have to make the choice – smart team member or sheep.

In truth nothing works as well as plain old-fashioned assertiveness. It is plain and straightforward and there is no need to play games or manipulate anyone. Just tell them straight: 'I am very busy, could this wait until later?'

thinking smart

CLOSED DOORS SIGNAL BUSY PEOPLE

Keep your office door closed to indicate 'no interruptions' (tell people you need to be left alone when the door is shut, assuming you don't work in an open-plan office). However, this works only if you give them enough time when your door is open – you can't leave it shut permanently.

THE SPARE CHAIR

If you keep a spare chair in your office for visitors make sure it is always piled high with folders and paperwork. If you want the visitor to stay, you clear it off. If you don't want them to stay, you don't. They then have to stand and will leave quicker as you've made it uncomfortable for them.

USING HAND SIGNALS

You can stop people dead in their tracks if you use hand signals. They may ignore a verbal request not to come in but few people can resist the non-verbal hand thrown up with palm outwards and arm fully stretched out. This is a pretty universal signal for 'come no closer, I may be dangerous' – and it works. If you accompany it with the verbal message 'Not now, I'm awfully busy', you have lessened the danger signal but it is still effective and moderately polite. If you do it while looking down at your desk at something vital and important, you make it less effective but more polite, whereas if you look them in the eye it is almost impossible to ignore but more threatening. Try it. It works.

In truth nothing works as well as plain old-fashioned assertiveness. It is plain and straight-forward and there is no need to play games or manipulate anyone

SENIOR INTERRUPTERS

How often have you been close to finishing a piece of work when some senior person comes along and gives you something completely different to do which means you miss your deadline? Too often probably. If it's the same person who gave you the original work to do, you have to say, 'That's fine but you do realise that if I have to complete this now I shan't be able to hand in the budget proposals on time?' They may well say, 'Oh, I'm sure you'll cope'. Don't stand for it. Emphasise the fact that you'll miss the deadline. 'No, I'm serious. I can't do both. There simply isn't the time.'

thinking fast

GETTING THEM OUT FAST

OK, so you let in an interrupter and they've got their feet under your desk. How are you going to shift them? Easy. Stand up and walk around a bit. It makes people feel uncomfortable to hold a conversation with someone who keeps moving around. If you make it uncomfortable for them then the chances are they will go somewhere else and interrupt someone else.

If it's another senior person giving you work to do say, 'That's fine but can you clear this with Michael first as I did promise him the budget proposals this afternoon and I simply can't let him down'. Let them fight it out, let them prioritise your time and don't try to please everyone all the time – you can't, you only have one pair of hands. If they are senior to Michael and simply tell you to get on with it, then tell Michael immediately that you can't meet his deadline because you've been overruled. That gets you off the hook. If they get cross, tell them to take it up with the other person and that you are helpless as you've been diverted.

thinking fast

JUST LEAVE

Why not just leave if you can't stand the interruption? Just say, 'I've got to go, I promised to see Sandy and I'm late already'. Chances are they will be gone by the time you get back. Or pick up some papers and say, 'I've got to go and photocopy these urgently, I'll be back in a while'.

FOR NEXT TIME

Get yourself a reputation for being frightfully busy all of the time. Make sure that all business tools such as e-mail are used for business only and not for gossip, humour, socialising or flirting. Be serious and smart. Make full use of your voice-mail facility and use it to avoid constant phone interruptions.

Deal directly and firmly with people dropping in or staying for too long. Practise your assertive techniques — see Chapter 3. Be polite at all times, but you are allowed to be brusque and businesslike — after all, it's what you are there for.

Get yourself a reputation for being frightfully busy all of the time

3 problems with other people

It's a fact of life, there are some pretty unpleasant characters out there. And you will run up against quite a few during your working life. They will cause you a lot of stress. What you need – and need now and fast – are ways of deflecting them. You can't make them go away. You can't kill them – well, not legally anyway. If they are causing you stress then what you need are ways of easing that stress rather than looking for ways of getting rid of them. You can't run or hide from all the unpleasant problem people in this world – that is unrealistic and impossible. Remember, if you can't change the situation (the problem people) then change your response (how you deal with the stress they cause).

ACCEPTANCE

Right. First things first. Let's clear up a popular misconception about difficult colleagues and bosses. You can't change them no matter what you do. That is a fundamental principle. So ditch that zealot's desire to reform them, improve them and generally make them more like you – which of course is rational, calm and always pleasant. Leopards cannot change their spots. You can't change a difficult person. All you can do is make their behaviour less stressful to you – and we'll certainly learn how, now.

None of us is perfect

When we think we can change another person we get irritated by them if they won't change. Once we accept they can't change we become more accepting. And once you stop trying to change people they realise you accept them for what they are and they too become less stressed – they have no need to feel angry or resentful. Also bear in mind that someone, somewhere sees you as a problem person. None of us is perfect. Our behaviour rubs someone up the wrong way.

YOU CAN BE DIFFICULT TOO

So how are you difficult? Try to analyse yourself objectively and see where your behaviour could be construed as difficult or unpleasant. It might be your mother who sees you as difficult because you never phone, or your partner who says you never clear up after you've finished cleaning your motorbike engine in the kitchen, or a colleague who resents the way you always get them to fix the photocopier even though they know you could do it if you really wanted to. You see?

NIL ILLIGITI CARBURUNDUM

This is an excellent motto for all of us at work. Roughly translated it is *don't let the b*****ds grind you down*. Don't let them. Set that as a personal challenge. No matter what they do, you will refuse to rise to the bait, get riled, get irritated, lose your rag/cool or take it too seriously. No matter what they throw at you, you simply rise above it and remain aloof and uninvolved. You come in, get the job done and go home. In between you remain Zen-like and detached.

RECOGNISING DIFFICULT PEOPLE

So now you know you can be more tolerant, but how can we build on this new tolerant approach? How can we persuade people that, if they can't change themselves, they might change their behaviour? Well, you're going to have to do some work here. First we are going to have to recognise some of these difficult people – identify the enemy before you load your gun.

 The problem person who always seems to know more, know better, uses jargon.

 The problem person who constantly criticises you.

 The problem person who never asks your opinion and makes decisions over your head.

 The problem person who overstretches your goodwill by asking for too many favours.

 The problem person who puts you down in front of other people.

 The problem person who settles arguments by losing their temper.

These are the main ones who, research has shown, drive us mad. Now we have identified them we can load our gun. And the bullets invariably are … assertiveness. Most of the problems these people generate will evaporate if treated effectively with a more assertive approach. Bear in mind we aren't judging these people. They aren't actually problem *people* at all. They are people who give us *problems* which cause us stress. Once we deal with the *problem* – and we must concentrate on this aspect – we can cope with and tolerate the people so much more calmly and reasonably.

BEING TREATED WITH RESPECT

Being assertive is about treating people equally and acknowledging your right to be treated with respect and courtesy yourself. They may be senior to you but you still have the right to be treated with respect, and if they aren't respectful then a few assertive techniques will quickly put them straight. Assertiveness isn't about aggression – far from it. It is about being confident enough to state your position and to get people to listen to you. It is about encouraging respect rather than demanding it. Assertive people are confident enough to be honest, to stand their ground and to have their opinion taken seriously.

1   Being honest – you are allowed to say what you think. It's as simple as that. This means that you can criticise people as long as you do it fairly and aren't rude or personal. You can begin this simply enough by just saying, 'I disagree' or 'I don't think your idea is workable'. Take it easy at first, but it gets easier as you practise it.

2   Standing your ground – easy one this just so long as you practise the scratched record technique. They want you to do something which you feel you can't. Easy. Just say, 'I'm afraid I can't do that'. Then when they put the pressure on merely repeat, 'I'm sorry I can't do that'. Now it's a question of whose nerve breaks first – and it ain't gonna be you 'cos you've got this book as your back-up. Just keep repeating it like a scratched record stuck in a groove and they'll back down first. Assertiveness can be pretty intimidating in a nice way.

3   Being taken seriously – you have to express yourself in a calm and reasoned way. It's no good being unpleasant or confrontational. All you have to do is express yourself assertively by saying, 'I feel ... when you ...' This way you won't provoke anyone but you will be taken seriously, as in 'I feel uncomfortable when you swear in the office'.

Most of the problems these people generate will evaporate if treated effectively with a more assertive approach

Assertive behaviour doesn't get rid of all your problems but it can effectively deal with quite a lot that are caused by the so-called problem people – the ones who create problems by their behaviour being less than it should in a modern, civilised working environment.

One of the essentials of assertive behaviour is remaining calm at all times. Problem people often feed off others' anger or irritation or defensiveness. If you are calm, rational and confident there is simply nothing for them to gain. If they can't rile you they may leave you alone and find a more usable victim.

EXPRESSING HOW YOU FEEL

That doesn't mean you can't express your emotions. Letting someone know how you feel is fine, but do it verbally, rather than with tears, hysteria, rage, punching or door slamming. It is so much more effective and productive to say, 'I feel very angry when you reprimand me in front of junior colleagues' rather than flouncing out of the office, sulking and slamming the door behind you. Both ways lets the person know you are angry, but saying it with words is so much more grown-up and will get much better results.

If someone starts hurling abuse at you it is easy

to get defensive and retaliate by shouting back. But it simply makes things worse. By remaining calm you stay focused. You keep a clear, objective perspective and can remain assertively in control. This gets you what you want quicker and more effectively. It is the smart approach.

ASSERTIVE FEEDBACK

Do it now. You can't wait until you're at breaking point before resolving issues. That's like only braking just before you hit the pedestrian – you might miss them, but then again you might not. It's too risky, too much of a gamble. Better to brake long before there is any real chance of killing them. Same with conflict. Resolve it before you kill them.

thinking smart

11

JUST THE ONE

If you want to change a difficult person's behaviour you can only attempt to change one thing at a time otherwise they will suffer from overload and resist all attempts to improve them. If they are negative, rude and petty, pick one. Try to change that particular bit of stressful behaviour towards you. Once you have accomplished that you can move on to the next bit. But don't attempt to build Rome in a day.

If someone starts hurling abuse at you it is easy to get defensive and retaliate by shouting back. But it simply makes things worse

STAYING CALM

It is essential to stay calm. But what if you can't? What if you really feel like bursting into tears or taking a swing at someone? Then leave the room. Say something like, 'I don't feel I can handle this at the moment' and then leave. If you can't leave then shut up and count to ten under your breath while practising one of the relaxation techniques described in Chapter 5. If you can't speak calmly, don't speak at all. If you feel like punching someone, sit on your hands.

for next time

FOR NEXT TIME

Make sure you aren't trying to change people, only their behaviour towards you. It is a lot less stressful if you start out being more accepting – we can't all be perfect and we have to make allowances.

Learn to recognise problem people – by their behaviour. Once we can see that it is their behaviour rather than their basic character, we can work towards alleviating the stress their behaviour causes us.

Get a copy of *fast thinking: difficult people* and read it thoroughly – to be prepared for the difficult person is half the battle.

It is a lot less stressful if you start out being more accepting – we can't all be perfect and we have to make allowances

4 problems with tricky types

There are some tricky types of behaviour that we need to look at in more depth – but quickly. I know you want instant solutions to all this stress, but first we have to understand what it is that is stressing you, and why. Once we have a guidebook we'll find our way a lot quicker. Without looking at the map we might wander in circles for too long. More haste less speed, and all that.

There are certain tricky behaviour types that nearly always drive us insane, and ones we're likely to encounter quite often:

- ▶ **angry people**
- ▶ **sulky people**
- ▶ **emotional blackmailers.**

ANGRY PEOPLE

We all get angry some of the time. And some anger is quite justified. But people using anger as a weapon to get you to do what they want you to do is unforgivable. So we have two types of anger, justified and strategic, and the ways we have of dealing with them are different.

Justified anger

This is anger that isn't being used as a weapon to get you to act in a certain way but the sort of anger that results from a serious situation. I'm sure it's never happened to you, but consider the team member who, by their thoughtlessness, has just put a major contract in jeopardy. Now the team leader is quite right to be angry and to make a scene – justified anger. They are angry for a good reason and if it is you they are ranting at, you had best listen – and listen carefully. Hear them out and they will calm down. Show them you sympathise with their point of view and that you realise the seriousness of the situation. Don't try to justify your actions at this point. It will just sound as if you are making excuses.

What do angry people actually want?

What angry people want, usually, is a result – an instant response to their anger. You've just upset the most important client you've got. It's no use saying, 'Sorry, I was tired and have been overworking lately and I snapped at them'. What the team leader wants to know is what you are going to do about it – NOW! Better to say, 'Look, I know I've upset them but I'll phone them right now and apologise'.

The justifiably angry person needs you:

- ▶ **to listen to why they are angry**
- ▶ **not to make excuses**
- ▶ **to suggest remedial action to rectify the situation immediately.**

Facing someone who is angry with you – and justifiably so, you've just cancelled their holiday and they'd booked to take their family to Tenerife for ten days – is frightening, upsetting, confrontational, stressful (extremely) and intimidating. But remember they are entirely justified in being angry. They want and expect you to do something to dissipate that anger. Getting angry yourself will only make it worse. Telling them not to be so silly

USING ASSERTIVE FEEDBACK

If you are going to confront someone directly with their annoying behaviour, you need to handle it carefully. They will feel uncomfortable and even shocked. You need to be supportive and calm. You really should pick a time when they are most open to listening to what you have to say and are not rushing off to lunch or going home. You need to make sure you are both private and uninterrupted by anyone else. Don't pussyfoot around the subject or be too dramatic. State your case simply and firmly. You have to identify clearly what behaviour stresses you and how it can be changed. But you also need to have an end goal in sight – what it is you want to happen in future. It is no use merely saying, 'You annoy me'. You have to say how they annoy you and under what circumstances, how you want them to stop annoying you, and suggest ways they can do this. You must also explain why their annoying you is counterproductive: 'I feel annoyed when you interrupt me at meetings and would prefer you not to. I cannot finish what I am trying to say which means my opinions are not being heard by the other team members and I feel that because of this my contribution is being overlooked. In future could you please refrain from interrupting until I have finished what I am saying. How does that sound to you?' And then allow them to have their say.

What angry people want, usually, is a result – an instant response to their anger will certainly inflame things. Laughing at their anger will get you a punch on the nose. You have to remain calm, listen to them and put things right.

Strategic anger, on the other hand, has to be treated differently.

DEALING WITH PUT-DOWNS

Being put down in public is stressful unless you are thick skinned. You must act and think fast to deal with this effectively. When someone says something derogatory about you directly in front of colleagues, you should immediately respond by saying, 'I'm sorry, but I feel hurt by that comment. What do you mean?' If they respond by saying they were 'only joking', don't let it go. Acknowledge their response and repeat your feeling. 'It may have been a joke to you but I feel hurt.'

If the derogatory comment is indirect – 'This project is going badly' – ask outright, but not aggressively, if it is you who is being blamed or held responsible. 'Are you implying it is my fault?' If they are then they will have to justify it. But you will have drawn attention to their comment and made others aware that they are being unfriendly or putting you down.

If you feel you can't be calm at the time then use the assertive feedback technique later when you are more in control of your feelings.

Strategic anger

Now I'm sure we are all reasonable people and can understand justified anger, but strategic anger? That's a different kettle of fish entirely. Strategic anger is someone using anger to frighten you so you will do what they want. It is very stressful to work around someone who uses this technique to get their own way. It's unforgivable and inexcusable. If you give into them once you're sunk. If they think it works – a bit like a child having a tantrum, in fact exactly like a child having a tantrum – they will use it again and again. And not only with you but with anyone else they come into contact with. You will need all your assertive skills to counteract this one.

Strategic anger is used by people who are immature and haven't grown up. Like children they can be dealt with effectively by you, as a sort of surrogate parent, being firm and not giving in to it. There are several ways to deal with strategic anger.

- ▶ Refuse to allow yourself to be shouted at – you deserve better. If anyone rants at you, be assertive and say, 'I don't appreciate being shouted at and I shall leave the room if you don't control your temper'.

- ▶ If they carry on shouting, do what you have said you would – leave the room. Remain calm and say, 'I shall come back when you have calmed down'. If their anger leaves you upset and you find it difficult to talk, just leave the room.

 Whenever they get angry and shout, leave the room. Don't argue back, don't explain or make excuses, don't justify or rationalise – just get up and leave the room. They will quickly learn that they aren't getting the response they want and will have to change their behaviour. If they were a child you could send them to their room. But they aren't so you have to walk away and, by doing this, leave them in their room. This lowers your stress levels considerably. By not getting involved you remain outside their game and thus unstressed.

SULKY PEOPLE

God, don't you just hate them? You say the slightest thing wrong and they clam up for days, turn away when you come in, refuse to answer your questions, turn their back on you. But they are sulking because they want you to know how upset they are. It's unfortunate that they choose such a childish way of doing so. Now I know most of us sulk from time to time, but what we are talking about here is the office sulker – someone who does this so often it stresses you right up. There are a couple of useful techniques to help you combat this – and reduce your stress levels.

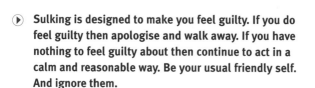

- ▶ Sulking is designed to make you feel guilty. If you do feel guilty then apologise and walk away. If you have nothing to feel guilty about then continue to act in a calm and reasonable way. Be your usual friendly self. And ignore them.

- ▶ If you persist in trying to get them to talk or be nice to you they have won. You mustn't give in to them. Just continue to ignore them and stop worrying about it. It is their stuff and you needn't get involved in their game. Pretend you haven't noticed and you've stolen their thunder.

- ▶ Don't make things worse by being cross with them, or indeed acknowledging in any way that their behaviour is affecting you in the slightest. Continue to behave completely normally.

- ▶ If you do have to make contact for work reasons and you know they are going to give you the silent treatment – and thus raise your stress levels – you have to be prepared to be assertive and play a waiting game. Ask them the necessary question then wait for their answer ... and wait ... and wait. Force them to break the silence by being resolute. Don't ask again. Just wait. One of you has to crack first and the onus is on them to reply. Deep down they know this and will be forced to respond. Human nature will not allow them to remain silent indefinitely. You only have to show them once that you are prepared to hold your ground longer than them and they won't use this technique on you again. *Ipso facto* your stress levels go down one notch.

11

DEALING EFFECTIVELY WITH TROUBLEMAKERS

There is no right or wrong way to deal with difficult situations caused by difficult people. You have to discover what works for you. Here are a few suggestions to add to your assertive repertoire.

- Ignore them and rise above it.
- Accept it and see the stress it causes as a personal challenge.
- Stand your ground and be assertive – declare what it is you want and what you expect from them in the way of reasonable behaviour.
- Complain to a senior person and get them to deal with it.
- Ask for help from a friend or close colleague – they may come up with a solution you have overlooked.
- Change your own behaviour to minimise the problems.
- Try to avoid all contact with the problem person.

EMOTIONAL BLACKMAILERS

There are few things more stressful than someone blackmailing you emotionally. 'Oh, please do this report for me or I shall be in such trouble'; 'Please could you handle the Gibson account as I feel so tired'; 'Could you do this discipline interview for me as they terrify me?' I'm sure you know the sort of thing. People getting you to do things for them because they don't want to do them themselves but instead of just being honest and saying that they put emotional pressure on you. It is a technique designed to make you feel bad, make you feel like a heel if you don't. It's manipulative and is used to make you feel guilty or sorry for them. Don't give into it. It is stressful and you need to be assertive to counteract it.

- ⏵ If someone asks you to do something that is in any way engineered to make you feel guilty then you must recognise it as emotional blackmail and refuse to respond. You have to acknowledge that this behaviour simply isn't fair on you and you thus have the right to refuse. If someone is prepared to try it on with you, they don't deserve your time or attention. You are being used. You are being unfairly stressed.

- ⏵ Simply refuse. Say, 'I'm sorry I can't do that'. If they come back with more of the same unreasonable emotional blackmail, adopt the scratched record technique – 'I'm sorry, I can't do that.' 'I'm sorry, I can't do that.' 'I'm sorry, I can't do that.' 'I'm sorry, I can't do that.' Don't allow them to make you feel guilty. It is them who is behaving unreasonably, not you.

- ⏵ Normally you shouldn't confront people with their chosen technique but this is one case where you can usually get away with it. You can say, 'You're not trying to emotionally blackmail me, are you?' As long as you do this with a laugh and are friendly they won't take offence and they will be brought up short once they recognise you have sussed them out.

WHAT ABOUT THE BOSS?

Ah, but I hear you ask, 'What about my boss? Surely I can't practise these assertive techniques on them without getting the sack?' Oh yes you can. Just because they are your boss doesn't mean they can treat you badly. You are entitled to respect, courtesy and equality. If you aren't getting it, you have to do some work to make sure you do. And there is a whole raft of legislation to make sure they don't sack you for simply being assertive and to ensure you are treated properly.

OK, so you want quick techniques to lower your stress levels when confronted with the unreasonable boss. Let's practise fast thinking and go for it. There are basically only three problematic types of boss who are likely to raise your stress levels to an unreasonable degree.

The control freak – they won't let you do a single thing without checking it first or making you report everything you do to them or breathing down your neck constantly. The only way to deal with them is to find out what their game is. And you can only do that by asking. Be bold. Be confident. Simply say, 'I feel you don't trust me to do my job properly. Is there a problem?' If there is, they'll tell you and you can then take their concerns on board and reassure them that you will improve/ change/be more efficient, – whatever it is they are worried about. You can also watch how they work and tailor your own work to fit in more with the way they always do things and thus they'll know they can trust you more.

If there isn't a problem they'll back off a bit, for a while. Then when they start breathing down your neck again you can go back and say, 'I've noticed you're monitoring my work very closely. Is there a reason for this?' Once you've done this a couple of times they'll back off completely, or at least as much as they can. Again remember you can't change them – they're a control freak – but you can change their behaviour towards you and thus lower your stress levels.

- **The absent boss** – they're never there when you need them. They never make decisions in time for you to do your job properly. They put things off. They prevaricate and hedge. They might as well not be there. They cause considerable stress. Again you have to be assertive to deal with them. Whenever an incident crops up when you could have done with them around, make a point of going to them and saying, 'I really needed a decision on the Wolffe report but I couldn't get hold of you in time. What do you suggest I should do if this crops up again?' And be ready with a suggestion of your own: 'Perhaps I could sign these reports in your absence, what do you think?' Try to see things from their point of view. Perhaps they are indecisive because they are frightened of taking charge. In which case by offering to take some of the burden off their shoulders they may well be grateful. If they are simply absent because they are lazy or too busy elsewhere, you again need to be assertive. Say to them, 'I can't do my job properly when you aren't around to supervise the invoicing procedure. What do you suggest I do if I can't get hold of you?'

And again be ready with a suggestion. What would help? 'Should I ask Mike in accounts if you're not available?' Usually they won't like you going to someone else and will say, 'No, I'll make sure I'm more available, you can always page me'. What you mustn't do is fume silently, stressfully. It is *their* absence that is causing *you* the stress, so field the ball back into their court. Make them do something about it. Don't pressurise them, just be assertive. Explain the problem and suggest ways of getting round it.

(▶) **The boss who knows best** – they don't listen to anyone else's point of view, why should they when they're always right? They like to shout a lot because they know best; they won't listen to criticism; they make decisions which everyone knows are wrong but they can't be told as they are always right. Tricky customer this one.

Again you have to be assertive but also clever. Don't try telling them they are wrong; instead ask questions. 'So, if I've understood you correctly, we ignore the company invoicing procedures for the Watson account. But what happens when the auditors ask about it?' 'If we change the way we induct the new staff what will happen when they need…?' 'I think I've got my head around this but could you just explain how that overtime stuff works on a bank holiday?'

By asking questions you get them to see where there may be an error in their thinking rather than confronting them with their mistakes. Of course if they *are* always right you needn't do anything. And as for them shouting or being in any way abusive, you just use all the standard assertive techniques – stand your ground and refuse to be browbeaten.

FOR NEXT TIME

Practise being assertive. Start off with the little things and work up to the really big, stressful situations. Express how you feel. Practise being honest. You are entitled to be treated with respect and have your opinions taken seriously. Speak your mind. Stay calm and leave the room if you feel too stressed.

Learn to spot the difficult boss further up the ladder so you can avoid working with them in the future if possible. Or try to get on the right side of them now, and then when the job comes of taming them, you'll be quids in.

Practise being assertive. Start off with the little things and work up to the really big, stressful situations. Express how you feel

5 work stress

I know, I know. You want quick and easy solutions to all your work overload problems. OK, we'll see what we can do as quickly and as effectively as possible. There simply isn't time – we are thinking at the speed of life, after all – to change jobs, retrain everyone around you to give you less to do or to supply you with an extra pair of hands. What we can do is give you some pointers and techniques to relieve the stress right now.

Fast and effective solutions

Research has shown that being overworked is one of the main causes of stress, along with difficult people (we've dealt with them) and incompetent work colleagues. But research has also shown that in the majority of cases too much work isn't the real problem, although it is given the blame. In fact, it is often poor time and work management that is the problem. What we need are fast and effective solutions – now.

One of the simplest ways of easing the stress of too much to do is organisation. If you effectively organise what it is you have to do you will see the wood for the trees a little more clearly. We are all guilty of it – stuff on e-mail to respond to, lists of tasks to do later, stuff in our head, Post-it notes attached to reports to be answered (and even just read in some cases), other stuff stored on the computer. What we need is a central file of what needs to be done, a simple list stored in one place with everything on it.

PRIORITISING YOUR WORK

Once you have sorted out your work more logically you can then prioritise it – do what is important first and things that are less urgent later. So what you need is a piece of paper. Yep, that old stuff. Forget computers, forget personal notebooks, forget business organisers. Just get a piece of paper. Now gather up all the tasks you have to do. You may need to print out the e-mails, make a note of the file that needs editing, add a note about the report you've got to read, jot down the people you've got to contact about the Johnson order – that sort of thing. This new central list doesn't have to contain much except short notes:

Forget computers, forget personal notebooks, forget business organisers. Just get a piece of paper

 **Answer Peter's e-mail**

▶ **Collate the sales brochures**

▶ **Phone Tony and Alice about the sales meeting**

▶ **Prepare the departmental report for Stanley**

▶ **Check with the auditors when they are coming**

▶ **Cancel the Friday staff meeting**

You don't have to specify why each of these tasks needs doing, just that they are in your pending tray waiting for you to take action on them.

Now you can group these items. If there are four which need a written response, group these together and allocate some time to sit down and do writing. If there are five which require a phone response, allocate some phone time. It makes sense to make all your phone calls at the same time rather than one phone call and then write one report and then send an e-mail and then make another phone call. You'll never know where you're supposed to be or what you're supposed to be doing if you jig about all over the place. No, the smart thing to do is save up tasks that require a special service such as telephoning and do them all at the same time.

Then you can prioritise these tasks. Maybe the Taylor report has to be read and commented on by lunchtime but the e-mail to Peter about next year's sales conference can wait until later in the day or even in the week. Well, it's pretty clear which needs your attention. But if you are going to sit down and read that damned report then you might as well read those other things at the same session. And you can then write several memos in the same session as it saves time. If you are already at your computer and have a word processing package open and available you might as well write everything you have to today.

This central list will become your saviour. Every morning update it. Cross out things you did yesterday and add new things that have to be done today. You can extend the idea to carrying a small notepad and rip out a page each time you complete all the tasks on it – very satisfying. Once you get into the habit of writing everything down in list form you will find your entire workload becomes much less stressful.

Once you get into the habit of writing everything down in list form you will find your entire workload becomes much less stressful

Now you have your list you can begin to option it — do what you need to and option the rest. Really there are only four options:

- ▶ **do it**
- ▶ **delegate it**
- ▶ **defer it**
- ▶ **dump it.**

Let's have another look at your list:

1   Answer Peter's e-mail

2   Collate the sales brochures

3   Phone Tony and Alice about the sales meeting

4   Prepare the departmental report for Stanley

5   Check with the auditors when they are coming

6   Cancel the Friday staff meeting

1   Answer an e-mail. Peter only wanted some research figures on German car sales for his report for next year's conference and that is ages away. We can pull the figures out when we have a spare five minutes – *defer*.

2   Collate the sales brochures. We can get Jimmy in despatch to do that – *delegate*.

3   Phone Tony and Alice. We can do this when we are making our phone calls – *do it*.

4   The departmental report. Stanley has now been posted to Newcastle and his replacement isn't due for six weeks and is unlikely to require a similar report – *dump it*.

5   Check with the auditors. Another one for our phone session – *do it*.

6   Cancel the Friday meeting. Urgent – *do it*.

Once you've gone through this process a couple of times it gets very fast and very efficient. All you have to do is collect all the delegation tasks and dish them out. Then decide on the deferment times and make a note of them in your diary – don't let them get forgotten as they are only being deferred.

Option your 'to do' list and allocate times for each one. As for the dump it list – well it doesn't take but a second to do that, does it?

TAKING ON MORE WORK

So we've sorted out our tasks and nicely completed a few when the boss strolls in and demands we do something else. This throws out our schedules and drives us insane; it rockets our stress levels and makes us think of resigning. But no. Hold on a minute. Are we reacting properly? When the boss hands us a new piece of work and says, 'Try to get this done by Friday morning, will you?', what do we say? How do we react? And what is the fast thinking way?

Most of us meekly accept the new work and fume silently. We mentally wring our hands and silently shout in desperation. Is this effective? No. Is this assertive? No. Does any of this lower our stress? No.

What we should do is:

- be honest
- make our position clear
- stand our ground.

So the correct response is, 'Yes, that's fine, but I will have to delay writing the Taylor report (honest). I would have preferred more notice of this assignment as I have just promised Mike the data for the video link by Thursday afternoon.' (Making your position clear.)

When confronted with assertive behaviour most bosses will begin to fluster, 'Well, see what you can do, anyway'. This simply isn't good enough. You're being fobbed off. You have to stand your ground. Again say, 'Yes, I can see what I can do but I have to warn you the Taylor report will have to wait until next week. I can probably get Jenny to give Mike his data but I really can't do both this and the report.' (Standing your ground.)

thinking smart

IF YOU'RE NOT PART OF THE SOLUTION, YOU MUST BE PART OF THE PROBLEM

In this day and age stress is a major killer. Everyone knows that, yet there is still a culture where it is put about that only the weak suffer from stress. Research shows this to be a myth and we must all work towards a stress-free environment, not a pressure-free one, we need the pressure to spur us on – and if we are contributing to the stress of others then we must become part of the solution. Create an area of calm around you at work and encourage others to do the same. *You* take the first step and others will follow.

Now your boss has to make a decision, prioritise *your* time. Instead of you having to work harder, longer and more stressfully, you have played the ball back into their court. They can:

- take away the new work and let you complete the report
- give you the new work and pass the report on to someone else
- demand you do both.

A good boss would see they were being unreasonable and increasing your workload beyond your capacity – you have only one pair of hands. Some will do the demanding bit which is very stressful and again you have to stand your ground. If they play the heavy 'I'm telling you, you have to do both', then you must continue to be assertive and not back down. 'I cannot do both. Do you have any suggestions as to how I could?' They are bringing you the problem. Keep feeding it back to them. See it as a bucket of stress. You don't want it, it's theirs. Hand it back and let them leave your office still carrying it. If you let them put it down, it's yours to keep.

thinking smart

THE NO-FAG FAG BREAK

We can't recommend smoking as a stress-busting technique, but smokers do often appear more relaxed. It might be nothing to do with the fags but the break they accompany. Try taking a no-fag fag break. Go and hang out with the smokers huddled in the rain under the bike sheds. Don't be tempted to indulge – that just causes more problems – but do take a break and get away, even if it's only for five minutes.

thinking smart

THREE SIMPLE THINGS

Research in America has shown that people recovering from heart attacks made better progress and had fewer subsequent attacks if they followed a three-pronged approach to life. They needed to learn a meditation/relaxation technique; they needed a belief system of some sort to support them; and they needed to belong to a social group of some sort – it could be as simple as going to night classes or having a few friends dropping in for a chat on a regular basis. The evidence also suggested that if we practised these three things in advance our likelihood of living to a ripe old age was greatly enhanced.

We can't recommend smoking as a stress-busting technique, but smokers do often appear more relaxed

MORE TIPS

If you want to ease your workload, get a copy of *fast thinking: work overload*. If you don't have time – as little as an hour will do – boy, are you stressed, so here are a few tips for cutting back, cutting down and easing up.

- ⓘ Set your objective before you start each task or project. It makes sense to know where you are going and what you intend to achieve *before* starting rather than muddling along and hoping you'll arrive at some satisfactory conclusion.

- ⓘ Prioritise your workload by organising tasks into groups – all the phone calls at once, the sort of thing that we've just looked at.

- ⓘ Delegate, delegate, delegate. We all like to hang onto work because we don't trust anyone else to do it to our own high standards. But to work effectively we have to learn how to delegate. Once we start it is surprisingly easy to do it.

- ⓘ You don't always have to delegate an entire task or project but by golly you can often delegate part of it. Before you begin each task have a look at it and ask yourself, 'Which bits can I give away?' – and thus lower your work stress levels. Remember, you are part of a team, not a one-musician band. Get the others to help and lower that blood pressure.

- ▶ I know we all have deadlines but often a lot of tasks can be deferred successfully until we have more time, better resources or whatever.

- ▶ Try to get into work as early as possible. It's invariably quieter and you will get fewer interruptions. You will also get unhindered access to photocopiers and other equipment. You can then clear your desk of a lot of tasks and leave the rest of the day free for phone calls.

thinking smart

BUILD IN COCK-UP TIME

If delegation is a new thing to you and you find it hard to trust, invariably you will be saying to yourself, 'But what if they cock it all up? What am I going to do then? It will be too late to redo it all.' Simple answer is to build in cock-up time so that you have some contingency time if they do let you down. Not a lot but some to get you out of trouble. Once you become more trusting and used to delegating you can cut this cock-up time to an absolute minimum.

- ▶ Don't take work home with you. You need a decent break between finishing work and starting again – you need to recharge those batteries. Do try to stop work at a reasonable time and go home. It is better to get up early and start work than to finish late.

You need a decent break between finishing work and starting again – you need to recharge those batteries

IT MIGHT NOT BE WORK

As we go through life we all encounter a lot of stress that has nothing to do with work. But stress caused by events outside of work affects us at work – we aren't machines and we can't shut down our feelings that easily. Be aware that some events outside of work affect us to a considerable degree and be kind to yourself if you have recently been through any of the following:

- ▶ divorce or marital separation
- ▶ death of your spouse or any near relative or close friend
- ▶ recently getting married
- ▶ any sexual difficulties
- ▶ any serious illness or injury or major health worries
- ▶ pregnancy or recent childbirth (this applies equally to men and women)
- ▶ moving house
- ▶ children leaving home.

IDENTIFYING THE CAUSE OF YOUR WORK STRESS

We all get stressed and rush about chasing our tail, yet very often we fail to sit down and work out exactly where that stress is coming from, and then also fail to do anything about it. Once we can identify the cause of our stress we can take positive action to eliminate it. Take a moment now to identify your stress and then we can help resolve it. All you have to do is answer a few questions. Take note of the answers and too many yeses in any one group will help isolate the stress area.

Home/work stress

Do you take work home with you? Do you have difficulty switching off at home? Does your work place a lot of strain on your home life? Do you have trouble prioritising work and home? Is your partner supportive about your work? Are there a lot of factors affecting you outside work that are stressing you, such as divorce, a recent death in the family or kids going through difficult stages?

Job satisfaction stress

Are you happy or very dissatisfied with the money you earn? Are you doing a job that stretches you? Do you have good career and/or promotion prospects? Is the physical environment you work in pleasant? Would you say you have 'job satisfaction'? Do you suffer from work insecurity such as threat of redundancy?

SAYING 'NO' AND MEANING IT

When we complain that we have too much work to do often we have no one else to blame but ourselves. If we ain't saying 'no', what are we saying? Too often we say 'yes' when we really mean 'no'. We say 'yes' because we want to be liked or because we are afraid of getting into trouble if we refuse. But saying 'no' is a key step in reducing our stress levels. Here's how.

- ▶ Keep it short. Just say 'no' and avoid over-long rambling explanations as to why you are refusing.

- ▶ Keep it polite. Say 'no' and say it nicely, 'No, I'm sorry but I can't'.

- ▶ Be calm. Just say 'no' with a smile. Don't shout or lose control. A simple 'no' is sufficient rather than 'For ****'s sake no, no, no, NO!'

- ▶ Keep it honest. If you can and want to, then say 'yes'. Reserve 'no' for when you really mean it.

- ▶ Be open. You can express the fact that saying 'no' is difficult for you – 'Look, I find this very hard but I have to say no, I'm sorry.'

- ▶ Say 'no' and move on. Once you've said it you may have to leave the room to avoid any indication that you might change your mind. And once you've said 'no', stick with it. Don't go back and chew it over again. 'I know I said no but I might be able to squeeze it in, what was the date again?', that sort of thing.

▶ Saying 'no' gets easier. Once you've said it once or twice it becomes less confrontational. It's those first few times that are difficult. You can always practise at home, or with friends to use as a sounding board.

thinking smart

ENVIRONMENTAL STRESS

We spend a lot of time at work and we need to make sure we aren't getting stressed by our environment.

▶ Make sure you've got lots of fresh air.

▶ If your office has central heating or air conditioning you may find plants, a bowl of water or an ioniser helps.

▶ Create a relaxing personal space around you with photos of loved ones, mementos, colourful desk accessories, that sort of thing. Create a home from home around you to help you feel comfortable and relaxed.

▶ Try to sit near a window to get as much natural light as possible – artificial light is very stressful.

▶ Try to maintain a noise level around you of less than 85 decibels – too much noise is stressful.

Be calm. Just say 'no' with a smile. Don't shout or lose control. A simple 'no' is sufficient

Relationship stress

Is your relationship with others at work good? Is your relationship with your direct manager good? Do you get encouragement and support at work? Do you have colleagues you can confide in? Do you have good training and guidelines to follow? What's the general morale of your team members like?

Responsibility stress

Are you responsible for managing other team members? Do you have to take a lot of decisions and make a lot of plans? Do you have to deal with conflict on a regular basis? Is there a lot of work politics going on around you? Are you frightened of making mistakes? Do you have to attend a lot of meetings or make a lot of presentations?

Role stress

Do you have a lot of different hats to wear? Are you clear what is expected of you? Do you have clear objectives to work towards? Are you often asked to change the way you work? Do you have lots of variety and stimulation? Do you gets lot of feedback about your performance? Do you have more than one boss?

thinkingfast

YOU DON'T HAVE THE TIME TO GET ANGRY

OK, you may have the time to blow it actually. You can lose your temper and your cool, but you simply don't have the time to purge the results of such loss of control. The surge in adrenalin levels has to be dissipated; your blood pressure has to be lowered; all the physiological changes needed for the 'flight or fight' response have to be eliminated. You may have the time to lose your temper but you don't have the time to correct such a bout of anger. It is quicker to be assertive than to be aggressive.

thinkingfast

HOW DO YOU BREATHE?

I expect you'll reply, 'With my lungs, of course'. Yep, but do you know how to use your lungs properly? If you use your chest muscles to expand and contract your lungs it is a sign of stress. If you lower your breathing to your abdomen you will relax much more and allow much more air to enter the system, which cleans out all that carbon dioxide. You'll be physically refreshed as well as relaxed. Put your hands gently on your stomach and make them rise up and down as you breathe in and out. You can do this only if you relax your shoulders and neck muscles. See, feeling better already. Be aware of where and how you breathe and as your breathing rises so do your stress levels.

Workload stress

Do you have too much work to do? Do you work long hours? Do you have a lot of demands on your time? Do you have too little work to do? Do you have to meet a lot of deadlines? Are there a lot of time pressures involved in your job? Are you qualified to do your job?

thinking fast

DO THIS NOW

Find a quiet place where you won't be disturbed for a few minutes and sit down in a chair. Make yourself comfortable but alert. Close your eyes and let your breathing become slow and rhythmic. Relax and pay attention to what is going on in your mind. Don't try to focus it – merely listen in as if to a crossed line on the telephone. Listen to the sort of words your mind uses. Now think about any routine task you have to do every day. Listen to what your mind says if you suggest that you won't do this task again. Does it say you've *got* to do it? *Must? Should? Have to?* We stress ourselves when we believe we've *got* to do things. When we *want* to do something it is a lot less stressful than when we feel we've *got* to.

There, that didn't take long and I bet you learned quite a lot about where your stress is coming from.

Remember, there are no right or wrong answers, no right or wrong approaches. But once you have identified your stress area you can work towards eliminating that stress and enjoy the other areas.

thinking smart

11

THE 12 'DON'TS' IN ELIMINATING WORK STRESS

Here are the 12 things you really need to stop doing to help you eliminate that stress.

1. Don't take work home.
2. Don't be a perfectionist.
3. Don't forget to get a life outside of work.
4. Don't put things off.
5. Don't bottle up feelings.
6. Don't try to do everything yourself.
7. Don't forget to ask for support.
8. Don't get addicted to anything – fags, booze, medication.
9. Don't work without regular breaks.
10. Don't say 'yes' to everything.
11. Don't work too long hours.
12. Don't lose sight of your game plan – it's only a job after all.

We stress ourselves when we believe we've got to do things. When we want to do something it is a lot less stressful than when we feel we've got to

THE NEED TO BE LIKED

We all want to be popular and often say 'yes' to tasks because we fear being disliked or seen as difficult. But being liked isn't necessary to getting the job done. It is a bonus. What we need is self-esteem. We need to approve of ourselves. If we become a doormat for others we will possibly be liked but will think badly of ourselves. If we are assertive we might be regarded as being 'tough' but we improve our self-esteem considerably – and thus reduce our personal stress levels.

thinking fast

REDUCING STRESS NOW

Here's a quick method of relaxing and reducing stress right now. Sit in a chair and tense every muscle in your body – clench your fists; clamp your jaw shut tight; screw up your face; hunch those shoulders and neck muscles; knot that stomach; push down hard with your feet. Now let it all go. Flop sideways in the chair and feel the tension seeping away. Imagine yourself as a balloon with all the air leaking out. Go limp. Let go of everything and sit quietly for five minutes feeling the tension melt away.

The need to be successful

Yep, we all want to get on and be rich and successful. But at what cost? If our health suffers and our personal relationships go down the Swanee, what's the point of all that money and success? Better to ease off and enjoy where we are and what we've got right now.

The need for things to be fair

Life ain't fair. Things go wrong. Stuff gets dumped. S**t happens. Once we accept that life (and work of course) isn't fair we can make allowances for our mistakes and for the fact that at certain times we will be dumped on and be treated unfairly. It happens. Nothing's perfect.

The need to panic

We are all capable of intense imagination… 'What's going to happen? Surely the very worst is going to befall me? This is a disaster!' It isn't. The worst will always be less than expected. Excessive imagination is unproductive. Be realistic at all times, control what you can and let go of the rest.

Once we accept that life (and work of course) isn't fair we can make allowances for our mistakes

The need to blame others

'If they didn't make me so angry I wouldn't be so stressed.' Not true. We all choose to be angry or not. We are not passive victims in all this. Our moods are not ruled by others. We can choose to whistle in the face of adversity or to break down and sob. It is our choice and we need to recognise that.

The need to run away

Isn't it easier to get the hell out of it and avoid the confrontation? Possibly, but it does nothing for our self-esteem, our sense of achievement. Better to take the bull by the horns and face difficult issues and challenges. Then, when we succeed, we can be genuinely proud of ourselves and feel very good indeed.

The need to be stuck

'I can't change. I am the way I am. There is nothing I can do.' Yep, we all like to be dinosaurs. But like them we will become extinct if we don't learn and grow and change with the times. We need to be fluid in our thinking and work and thus bendable and supple. If we are stuck, we break.

The need to judge

We all like to set ourselves up as judges. 'If their behaviour was more like mine we would all get along a lot better.' But we are all different. If we adhere to a rigid code of conduct and judge others harshly if they digress from *our* chosen path, we suffer constant stress because people will always let us down. They let us down because we have set up a system for judging them in advance. Better to demolish the system and allow them to be themselves. Thus they will constantly surprise us with their capabilities and initiative and we will think better of them.

The need for fate to play its part

I'm sure we all do it. We wait for something to turn up. We assume things will get better naturally. We cast our lot in with fate and wait for fate to look after us. And then we get stressed when nothing better does turn up or fate fails to get us out of the jam. Better to take control, to plan, to be less passive and more dynamic. Take responsibility, be committed and make things happen yourself.

Better to take control, to plan, to be less passive and more dynamic. Take responsibility, be committed and make things happen yourself

HANDLING NERVES

Phew, we've certainly covered a lot of ground. And we've looked at the ways in which most people say they get stressed. But there is one last category that came out quite high in recent research into stress – nerves. We all work with others, have to attend meetings, make presentations and speak in public. If we find it all easy, then brilliant. But for most of us it can be difficult. Here are the top tips for easing nerves.

- ▶ **Preparation, preparation, preparation.** Yep, the three key things to do – prepare beforehand. If you are rehearsed, prepared and word perfect you will be less likely to be nervous. Being nervous is about making a fool of yourself. If you are wisely prepared you cannot appear foolish.

- ▶ It will never be as bad as you think.

- ▶ Don't hyperventilate. Breathe slowly and deeply, but not too much. Relax and let your neck and shoulders drop.

- ▶ Take it slowly, step by step. Concentrate on what you have to do and don't worry about anything else.

- ▶ Being nervous is part of life – it isn't life threatening, you won't die, you will survive. Feeling nervous is unpleasant but it is not harmful or dangerous.

- ▶ It is better to jump than not to jump – go for it, you can only improve, grow and develop. Being nervous is part of your growth. Accept it as a sign that you are being challenged and thus expanding in skill, knowledge and experience. Well done.

 ## for next time

FOR NEXT TIME

You may be stressed now and ready to take action to reduce it. But how are you going to make sure it doesn't creep back up again? To help keep stress levels low you can:

- ▶ make sure you have a network of friends around to sound off to
- ▶ maintain a proper routine of sleep and decent food
- ▶ set long-term goals and work constructively towards them
- ▶ manage your time effectively and don't fritter away time on non-essential nonsense – do what needs to be done and dump the rest
- ▶ enjoy the moment – take satisfaction from what you are doing right now rather than worrying about tomorrow or trying to rectify yesterday
- ▶ challenge yourself – see stress as a challenge, something to be successfully overcome. Throw yourself into the fray and survive! What could do more for your self-esteem than to say 'I did it!'

Being nervous is about making a fool of yourself. If you are wisely prepared you cannot appear foolish

de-stress in half an hour

OK, so you're stressed and have a spare half an hour to relax. Find somewhere comfortable to sit, preferably out of your office where you won't be disturbed. Follow this routine and then practise whenever you get stressed. Once you are ready you can begin by tensing your feet. Scrunch up your toes as tightly as possible for about five seconds. Then let go. Do this for each part of your entire body in the following order (tense for five seconds, then let go).

- ▶ **Feet – push down firmly – and let go.**
- ▶ **Ankles, calves, knees – tighten against foot pressure against the floor – and let go.**
- ▶ **Thighs – push down hard against the floor and then let go.**
- ▶ **Hands – clench into fists and then let go.**
- ▶ **Arms – tighten biceps and let go.**
- ▶ **Bottom – clench buttocks tightly and let go.**
- ▶ **Lower abdomen – push out firmly then let go.**

- ▶ **Stomach** – hold in, push out, then let go.
- ▶ **Chest** – expand firmly and let go.
- ▶ **Shoulders** – hunch up towards your ears as far as possible and let go suddenly.
- ▶ **Neck** – stretch up as far as possible, pull your chin down as far as possible, and let go.
- ▶ **Face** – scrunch up as much as possible (imagine you are eating a lemon) and let go.
- ▶ **Jaw** – clench your teeth together as hard as possible and let go.
- ▶ **Eyes** – screw tight shut and let go.
- ▶ **Forehead** – frown as deeply as possible and let go.

Go through this exercise in the order suggested. Basically you are just working up the body. You can, for added benefit, work your way down again. Remember to tense each muscle group for about five seconds and as tightly as you can. Remember to let go of the tension each time. As you release the tension, feel what happens to the muscles as they relax. Be aware of the difference between a muscle being tensed and being relaxed.

You can also do this exercise by tightening and releasing each muscle group twice if you are very tense. Or you can do it lying down – and don't worry if you fall asleep afterwards, you really are relaxed.

de-stress in ten minutes

So you're in a meeting and it's all getting too much or you're about to give an important presentation and you're feeling very stressed. You've got a spare ten minutes. What are you going to do? Well, getting up and leaving the office for ten minutes will chill you sufficiently to re-enter the battle ground with a fresh outlook.

- ▶ Get out into the fresh air for ten minutes and breathe deeply – use abdominal breathing (see page 83) – and switch off from the current problem.

- ▶ Close your eyes for a moment and think of a happy memory such as a fabulous holiday you had as a child.

- ▶ If you have the space, lie down on your back with your arms resting by your side in the classic 'corpse' position.

- ▶ Let everything relax.

- ▶ Close your eyes and imagine you are floating on a bed of air, totally relaxed, totally safe, totally unstressed.

Getting up and leaving the office for ten minutes will chill you sufficiently to re-enter the battle ground with a fresh outlook